SUMO

SUMO

*the
sport
and the
tradition*

by J. A. SARGEANT

CHARLES E. TUTTLE COMPANY
Rutland, Vermont   Tokyo, Japan

Representatives

For Continental Europe:
BOXERBOOKS, INC., *Zurich*

For the British Isles:
PRENTICE-HALL INTERNATIONAL, INC., *London*

For Australasia:
BOOK WISE (AUSTRALIA) PTY. LTD.
104-108 Sussex Street, Sydney 2000

Published by the
Charles E. Tuttle Company, Inc.
of Rutland, Vermont & Tokyo, Japan
with editorial offices at
Suido 1-chome, 2-6, Bunkyo-ku, Tokyo

Library of Congress
Catalog Card No. 59-5993

International Standard Book No. 0-8048-1084-2

First printing, 1959
Eighteenth printing, 1985

Printed in Japan

Table of Contents

ILLUSTRATIONS

CHAPTER 1

In Days Gone By

The West has its "sport of kings." Japan, in Sumo, has her "sport of emperors."

Tokyo's famous mecca of Sumo, the Kuramae Kokugi Hall, has a conspicuous royal box. When Emperor Hirohito takes his seat there, gazing in loving admiration on the colorful spectacle that unfolds before him, he is but following age-old tradition. With a difference, however. Nowadays the emperor goes to Sumo; in the old days Sumo went to him.

Even in ancient times the imperial court, the story goes, resounded with the stamping of the feet of the Sumo giants, and down the years the emperors as well as the great warrior-lords who ruled Japan during the Middle Ages have been ardent devotees of this manly sport. The first recorded and perhaps most famous bout of all time was one that astonished and delighted the eyes of the Emperor Suijin a few years before the opening of the Christian era. Nomi-no-sukune with his seven-foot-ten-inch frame, was a formidable opponent, but his rival, Taema-no-kehaya, after a Homeric struggle that seemed interminable and thrilled the hearts of the emperor and his court,

finally dealt him such a hefty and well-placed kick that he felled
him on the spot. This was quite in keeping with what went on in
those blood-thirsty days but, needless to say, in this more refined
Atomic age, violence of that sort is completely taboo.

With its imperial beginnings, Sumo certainly started out on the
right side of the tracks, but, curiously enough, the very first grand
tournament, or *basho,* was held in a temple compound, and temple
and shrine grounds continued to be one of the favorite sites for bouts
through the centuries. These religious and imperial ties probably
account to a large extent for Sumo's being adorned with so much
pageantry even today.

Professional Sumo is said to have originated in the sixteenth
century under the overlordship of the famous Oda Nobunaga; but
its colorful history of men of valor, real and legendary, dates back
further. We are told that about eleven hundred years ago there
was a muscle-man named Hajikami living in Omi, the present
Shiga Prefecture, who was so strong that the ordinary run-of-the-
mill wrestler could not handle him. He always won hands down
and took all the fun out of the sport, so one resourceful referee at
a contest in Osaka's Sumiyoshi Shrine obtained a coil of thick rope,
or *shimenawa,* and tied it around Hajikami's middle. To even
things up, it was announced that any man who could succeed in
touching the rope would be declared the winner. This, of course,
added some spice to the proceedings, but even at that Hajikami
remained undefeated. It is thanks to him that great white hawsers
still adorn the midriffs of the grand champions, or *yokozuna,* even
today (see Plates 5, 6, 12 & 13). Ironically enough, however, Hajikami was not proclaimed first grand champion. That honor was
reserved for another Sumo great, Akashi Shiga-no-suke, a figure

shrouded in mystery of whom there is actually no precise record available.

It seems that in the early part of the seventeenth century a great tournament was held at the imperial court in Kyoto. Akashi, the son of a samurai, defeated Nio Nidaya, of Nagasaki, to win the tourney and become the first official *yokozuna* in the history of Sumo. He reputedly stood over eight feet tall and weighed over four hundred pounds, but the figures are not official, and he has no doubt grown in stature with every passing generation. Not long after copping the title, he came up to Edo, as Tokyo was then called, and appeared at the Sasa-dera, a temple in Yotsuya, on the occasion of the first grand tournament ever held in the present capital of Japan.

We are on much firmer ground when we come to Tanikaze Kaji-no-suke, the fourth grand champion and possibly the greatest of them all. The son of a poor farmer of the Tohoku region in the north, he was born in 1749 and hailed from the neighborhood of Sendai, in Miyagi Prefecture. During a period of eight years in the ring he piled up the amazing record of 183 wins, 12 losses, and 25 ties, in a total of 220 bouts. That gives him an average of .938. His achievement of going through sixty-six bouts without a defeat has been bettered only by Futabayama's sixty-nine. In contrast to some of his legendary predecessors, Tanikaze was a mere six feet two inches in height, and his 344 pounds put him in about the same class as the modern pot-bellied Kagamisato. He finally succumbed, not to an opponent in the ring but to an attack of influenza and died in 1795 at the age of forty-six. A Japanese saying has it that "There never was the equal of Tanikaze, before or since." His name means "wind of the valley."

The next star in the ranks of the great was Raiden Tame-emon, a 370-pound six-foot-three-incher who wrestled at the end of the eighteenth and the beginning of the nineteenth century. His greatest feat was to win no less than twenty-five tournaments, seven of them in succession. Raiden holds the dubious distinction of remaining in the champion, or *ozeki,* slot for seventeen years; he was never elevated to the rank of grand champion because he roughed it up too much. The only man who could get away with that sort of stuff was the before-mentioned Nomi-no-sukune.

Coming to comparatively modern times, the two great wrestlers of the Meiji era were without a doubt Totaro Ume-ga-tani II (1878–1927) and Hitachiyama Taniemon (1874–1922). Ume-ga-tani chalked up a wonderful winning average of .920, but in fifteen tilts with his arch-rival Hitachiyama, his amazing technique seemed to be of no avail, and he managed to come out on top but thrice. Hitachiyama walked away with seven matches, and the rest were ties. Bouts between these two are said to have been really terrific, the greatest in modern Sumo. Ume-ga-tani, with his five feet six inches, tipped the scales at 335 pounds. Hitachiyama towered two inches above him, but was inferior in weight, being a measly 320 pounds.

Hitachiyama, the nineteenth *yokozuna,* was an all-time great. After attaining *maku-uchi* (inside-the-curtain) rank he lost only eight times in eighteen tournaments, spread over nine years. He was truly a stupendous personage of the period. He might indeed be called the prototype of the modern Sumo man, being the first Japanese wrestler ever to go abroad. In 1907 he visited the United States where he was presented to "Teddy" Roosevelt; he was accompanied by the present Dewa-no-umi, until recently head of the Japan Sumo Association. Visitors to the Sumo Museum at the Kuramae Kokugi Hall may see the top hat and walking stick that

Hitachiyama sported when he went to the States. Naturally, he took with him an apron, such as all Sumo wrestlers wear at the *dohyo-iri,* their daily ceremonial entry into the arena. But none has ever been graced with one like Hitachiyama's. It was studded with diamonds and was worth millions.

In throwing a few bouquets, one might consider Tanikaze, Hitachiyama, and Futabayama (Plate 1), of whom more anon, to be Sumo's great trio; but men like Terukuni, who in 1944 at the age of twenty-four became the youngest grand champion on record, should not be forgotten. The opposite sort of record was set up by the twelfth *yokozuna,* Jimmaku, in the mid nineteenth century. He was actually thirty-nine years of age when he attained the rank of grand champion, and he carried on long after that. These days, with six big tourneys a year, that kind of staying power is out of the question. It's like baseball. With all those night games there'll be no more like Ty Cobb or Eddie Collins, who carried on for over twenty seasons.

CHAPTER 2

Born Sumoists

It is a hotly debatable question whether or not baseball has supplanted Sumo as the national sport of Japan.

Undoubtedly in such great centers of population as Tokyo, Osaka, and Nagoya, one sees more youths with bat, ball, and glove than one sees practicing the land's ancient and traditional sport. In many parts of the country, nonetheless (particularly true in the case of the farming villages of the north and the fishing villages), the reverse is to be found. The rustic Sumo ring often takes the place of the urban baseball diamond.

There are quite a number of reasons for Sumo's popularity with the country boys, one being, of course, that the rural areas have enjoyed much less frequent contact with Western influences. In many districts feudalism is still rife, apparent if one but scratches the surface, and the great Japanese professional baseball squads in their provincial tours never touch these remote areas.

Another reason is economic. The farmers in the north eke out a bare living, the land is poor, crop failures are not uncommon. They have little money to spend on their sons' pastimes. Consequently, the boys take up the cheapest sport they can find. Sumo, of course, fills the bill perfectly. All that is required is a simple ring and a loin-cloth, and the latter, it is unnecessary to add, need not be studded with diamonds. Just something to spare the sensitivities of the country maidens.

Incidentally, it is no mere coincidence that so many of Japan's grand champions hail from Hokkaido or the northeastern districts, areas throughout the long winter under a blanket of deep snow, trudging through which strengthens the hips—a vital part of every wrestler's anatomy. The same thing may be said of youths from the mountains. It is natural that they should be able to develop stronger hips than the lads who walk only on the flat, non-hip-developing plains. In rowing, too, the hips come into much play. Thus, the sons of fishermen often turn out to be good wrestlers. The greatest sumoist of modern times, Futabayama—now retired and, under the name of Tokitsukaze, head of the Japan Sumo Association—is a fisherman's son from the Kyushu prefecture of Oita, in southwest Japan.

Of the three reigning grand champions only one, Tochinishiki (see Plates 6, 7, & 10), was born and brought up in a city. He is the son of a Tokyo umbrella-maker. The remaining two are from the snowy north, Chiyo-no-yama (Plate 5) from the northern island of Hokkaido and Waka-no-hana (Plates 8, 15 & 16) from Aomori, at the extreme northern tip of Honshu, Japan's main island. A similar proportion may be found among the lower-ranking grapplers. The life of the city slicker is evidently not conducive to the production of a great wrestler.

The Japanese race as a whole, however, may be said to be well adapted to the sport of Sumo. The reason is that the Japanese, if

I may be permitted to use such an ungraceful term, are rather "low in the water." By this I mean, of course, that they have been endowed by Mother Nature with long bodies and short legs.

In Sumo the point of balance or fulcrum must be as low as possible. It makes a man so much more difficult to topple. Generations of squatting on the *tatami* (straw mats used to cover the floor) instead of sitting on chairs have perhaps more than anything else developed the Japanese type of body. In this connection it is of interest to note that an improved diet through the increased intake of meat, bread, and dairy products, together with a greater use of chairs, is producing a taller and more massive breed.

A consequence of this has been a gradual raising of the standard required of Sumo novices. At the end of the Meiji era (around 1910) the requirement was a minimum weight of a little over 132 pounds. There was no limitation on height. By the beginning of the Showa period (1926) the standard had risen to about 160 pounds and a lad had to be at least five feet five inches in height before he could be accepted. Since May, 1957, the standard of height has been five feet seven inches and of weight 166 pounds. There can be little doubt that with the gradual improvement in Japanese physique these standards will go on rising.

The elephantine Odachi, who retired early in 1958, ranks with the Sumo giants of all time. He stepped into the ring at close to 390 pounds and tipped the beam at six feet four inches, a veritable colossus. And that's not all. He slimmed down from well over 400 pounds, the heaviest ever, maybe. Anyway, it's an enthralling question, with such monsters as Dewa-ga-take in the field. This lad, who got as far as *sekiwake* (junior champion) in the 1920's, towered to a height of six feet five inches and fluctuated in weight between 360 and 430 pounds. He was so strong that certain of the regular sixty-eight holds were barred to him after he had, accidentally of course, caused the death of an opponent in the ring. The Japan Sumo Association no doubt heaved a sigh of relief when this behemoth retired just before World War II.

As for height, the modern "Eiffel Tower" is the prognathous demoted champion, Ouchiyama, who can lay claim to six feet seven and one-half inches. But way back in the 1820's there was a wrestler boasting the picturesque name of Ozora (big sky) who really was a sky-scraper, if figures don't lie. He was a staggering seven feet three inches and would have been worth his weight in gold to any basketball team. The first grand champion, Akashi, who flourished in the seventeenth century, is said to have reached seven feet five inches. But this, like most facts about this gentleman, should perhaps be taken with a big grain of salt.

CHAPTER 3

The Road to Stardom

Taro, a farmer's son, is a hefty lad; at fourteen he already tips the scales at 165 pounds. There's no matching him for miles around; he can throw all his comrades with ease. A grand champion in the making, as everyone agrees.

One day, in the course of a provincial tour, a group of noted wrestlers from Tokyo reaches the neighboring town. The word is passed around that a boy called Taro is something out of the ordinary. Inquiries are made and, before he knows where he is, he is whisked up to the capital and installed as an apprentice in one of the great Sumo gyms. Here he will live in, with his food and pocket money provided by the master of the gym, a retired Sumo great. He will be given no salary, of course, for a number of years; first he must prove himself.

Taro's gym is located in the Ryogoku area of Tokyo, where are to be found by far the greater number of these institutions; for it was in this quarter that the great tournaments were formerly held, at the arena now known as the Kokusai (International) Stadium. There are about fifteen of these gyms scattered throughout Ryogoku. They

1. THE PRESIDENT: Tokitsukaze (ex-grand champion Futa-bayama), president of the Japan Sumo Association, is shown in Japanese attire standing at the entrance of the gym or training quarters of which he is the master.

2. SHIKIRI-NAOSHI: The two wrestlers here are engaged in *shikiri-naoshi,* which precedes a bout. They crouch, with fists firmly planted in the sand, studying each other intently. The referee, in the rear with fan upraised, regulates the proceedings.

4. THE MIGHTY FALLEN!: Lying like a pole-axed steer is the burly Tokitsuyama, the victim of Tama-no-umi's *hiki-otoshi,* which may be translated "pulling him down." The referee may be glimpsed in the rear, behind Tama-no-umi.

3. UTTCHARI: In this tactic the man underneath, in this case Koto-ga-hama, wearing knee supporter, digs in with his heels on the edge of the ring and with a quick twist of the body to the left sends his opponent Shimizugawa spinning out of the arena before he himself falls.

5. GRAND CHAMPION CHIYO-NO-YAMA: Chiyo-no-yama (center, with arms outstretched) is shown at the *dohyo-iri* with his *tachimochi* (left) holding the sword and *tsuyuharai* or attendant (right). Referee is at extreme left.

are nothing much to look at—just plain frame houses containing little more than the training ring itself and a large communal eatery. They house, all told, a total of approximately one thousand wrestlers. Taro's is one of the larger gyms so he finds himself a member of a squad of some seventy or eighty wrestlers, most of them apprentices like himself, but including the whole hierarchy of Sumo-dom right up to the champions and grand champions themselves.

The young hopeful has a hard life in front of him as he starts out on the road to fame. In the first place he is, in spite of recent attempts at democratization, in what may frankly be described as a feudalistic set-up. His status is not unlike that of a fag at an English public school, for he has to fetch and carry for his elders. in return for which they see to it that he gets to know the ropes.

Among his other multifarious duties will be scrubbing the backs of his superiors in the bath, combing and fixing up their hair-do when training is over, and doing all the cooking and the cleaning up of the establishment. And what do the women do, you may ask? The answer is simple; there are no women, apart from the master's wife. Sumo-dom is strictly stag.

Taro and his fellow-neophytes rise at the crack of dawn and, it might be thought, start off the day by downing a hearty breakfast. Nothing of the sort! There is no breakfast. The youngsters tumble out of the sack around five or six—before the streets are aired—clean up the ring, and get going with their warming-up exercises. Their elders, as befits their rank, lie abed a little later, but they too are usually on the scene by eight at the latest. The seniors put the youngsters through their paces, tip them off as to their faults, and so on and so forth. The master of the gym is mostly in attendance to keep a watchful eye on the proceedings, but in his absence this duty is delegated to the top-ranking wrestlers.

The entire forenoon is devoted to various forms of training and practice bouts—and all the while not a bite of food. Spartans they are indeed, but then they have to be. This is no life for a weakling, and if a lad can't stand the pace, he simply drops out. It's rough all right but Taro will not be bullied, for this regime, feudalistic though it may sometimes seem, is not militaristic. The life is tough, but not brutal; if a boy can't or won't learn, he won't get on. That is punishment enough.

Morning training done, the lads have to wait on their seniors at the mid-day meal, after which they can immerse themselves in the welcome tub and rub their manifold bruises, and then, at long last, help themselves from the common pot of stew. The meal over, Taro and his mates have the rest of the day to themselves and it can well be imagined that they make it a day of rest; indeed, with their energy used up and no money to burn, there's nothing else for it. If the lads wanted to kick over the traces they wouldn't have the wherewithal; for them wine and women just don't exist.

When Taro approaches the dizzy heights of stardom, possibly ten years later, and can afford to take unto himself a wife, he is allowed to reside in his own home, of course, for too many wives would clutter up the gym. During a big tournament, however, even the married wrestlers often prefer to move back into the gym for greater convenience. Perhaps, too, for greater ease of mind.

Incidentally, the Taros of the future will lead somewhat different lives from those of their predecessors for, in line with the gradual defeudalization of the sport, a Sumo training school has recently been established, to be attended by scrubs from the various gyms.

CHAPTER 4

Grand Tournaments

The basho or grand tournaments are the World Series of Sumo. Currently there are staged six grand tournaments a year—the New Year tournament, held in Tokyo, the spring tournament in Osaka, the summer and autumn tournaments in Tokyo, the July tournament in Nagoya, and the November tournament down in Kyushu at the city of Fukuoka. The two last-named are recent additions.

These joustings have a long history—and few would ever guess where the first one on record was held. It was in the precincts of a temple on the outskirts of the ancient city of Kyoto, a former capital of Japan. That was way back in the Kansei era (1789–1800). Only one tournament was held a year, and it could hardly be called official. And they wrestled only five days. Still, it was a beginning.

It was not until around the end of the Edo period (1868) that the one tourney became two. These were held in January and May, in Tokyo. Tokyo's first arena was, as in the case of Kyoto, a temple, by name, Sasa-dera. By this time the length of a tournament had increased to ten days. Then, as interest in the sport mounted, it became necessary to build a hall capable of accommodating all the fans, so in the forty-second year of Meiji (1909) the spacious Ryogoku Kokugi Hall (the present Kokusai Stadium) was opened, and for the first time Sumo had a home worthy of its long history.

The remark is sometimes passed that we moderns are sissies. But this can certainly not be applied to the sumoists. They started out with five-day tourneys, which, as we have seen, later went up to ten days. And then, in the fourteenth year of Showa (1939), fifteen-day tournaments were instituted. It is incontestable that a man has to be plenty tough to be pulled and pushed and flung around like a sack of coals for fifteen days on end. Things are just getting tougher and tougher for the lads.

And then, as if to make it all the harder, in 1948 Osaka was given its first big tournament, making three in all. Tokyo was handed an additional tournament in the autumn of 1953, and, to cap it all, Fukuoka was accorded the honor of putting on the big show from 1957 and Nagoya from 1958. One may think it's all pretty rough on the grapplers who, in days of yore, had to work only about twenty days a year. They don't really mind, though. And for a very good reason. They can make more dough, as will be explained later on.

A novice will make no more than a fleeting appearance in the great ring on the occasion of his first tournament. He will merely "drop in for a cup of coffee" on the first day only before a handful of spectators and then retire for the remainder of the proceedings. His name will not even appear on the official ranking list of the Japan Sumo Association, a Magna Charta-like screed written in hundreds of quaint Chinese characters, as in ancient times. When it does appear, it will be microscopic but will gradually loom large as he attains the dizzy heights of stardom. As his technique develops and he puts on weight, he will emerge more and more frequently—and later and later in the day.

A real, dyed-in-the-wool Scotsman would just love a Sumo tournament, for he could settle himself comfortably in his seat at six in the morning and still be there at six in the evening. Talk about getting one's money's worth! There has never been anything quite like it.

The ring the Tokyo novice finds himself in is laid out with *rakida* earth, specially brought in from neighboring Chiba Prefecture. The ring is two feet high and eighteen feet square at the base. Around it are placed a number of thick coils of straw forming a circle fifteen feet in diameter. All nice and soft to fall on—after the right kind of training, that is. From the four corners of the awning of the ring are suspended four huge tassels, signifying the seasons of the year, with a blue tassel on the east side, white on the west, black on the north, and red on the south. Until 1952 four large colored poles supported the awning. These, however, were found to interfere with the view of the sport and were replaced by tassels. The awning is now suspended from the roof of the hall by means of cables.

CHAPTER 5

Sumo Ranking

A grand Sumo tournament resembles a drama which opens quietly, the suspense being gradually built up as the play unfolds itself until the climax is reached. A tournament starts with the striplings in the early morn. As the day rolls on, higher and higher ranking sumoists take the stage until finally the grand champions make their appearance.

It is with the *ju-ryo* (ten *ryo*—an old Japanese coin—was their pay) wrestlers that the interest of by far the greater part of the fans begins to be aroused. This group of around fifty grapplers, immediately below the top-ranking *maku-uchi* men, starts wrestling early in the afternoon. They merit interest inasmuch as their bouts are the first to be given much notice in the vernacular sports papers.

Following the final *ju-ryo* tilt come the "Grand March of the Gladiators" and the "Triumphal Entry of the Grand Champions," later to be described in detail. Excitement mounts as, the ceremonial over, the top-rankers commence to take each other on. But first, a word or two as to ranking, as it concerns Sumo's highly exclusive *maku-uchi* group.

The *maku-uchi* group is sub-divided into *mae-gashira* (literally, "before the head") and *san-yaku,* the former composed of about forty-five wrestlers numbered *mae-gashira* 1, 2, 3, etc. *San-yaku* men are further divided into *komusubi, sekiwake, ozeki* (champion) and *yokozuna* (grand champion). Higher than that a wrestler cannot go. He is standing on Sumo's Everest. *Sekiwake* may be translated, perhaps, "junior champion, first grade," and *komusubi* "junior champion, second grade."

All wrestlers wear their hair done up in a queue, and one may recognize the approximate rank of a man by the elaborateness or simplicity of the queue. Tyros have their hair fixed in a plain top-knot or *chon-mage,* while the top rankers *(san-yaku)* affect the fashion termed *o-icho-mage.*

Nor should it be thought that this is all mere affectation or tradition. The top-knot acts as a buffer between the wrestler and the floor of the ring when he is brought to earth with such a thwack that his skull seems likely to be split in two.

Wrestlers are boosted or busted according to their achievements. A man who has a won-lost record of, say, twelve-three in the spring tournament may well find himself elevated from *mae-gashira* 15 to *mae-gashira* 9 for the summer tourney. And he'll probably be dropped six or seven rungs if all he can show is a three-twelve mark. An eight-seven record will probably lift a man but a single rung and a seven-eight score boot him down one.

Ascending the Sumo ladder is, as may be imagined, somewhat like climbing the Himalayas. Progress is fairly rapid on the lower slopes, but the higher one gets the rarer the air becomes, and the advance is at snail's pace. That is, if one is not actually driven back.

For this is what usually happens when a young hopeful attains the heights of *komusubi* for the first time.

With the laudable object of saving the best bouts—those between two grand champions or between grand champion and champion— for the end of the tournament, the gentlemen who arrange the programs find it necessary on the first two or three days or so to pit the *komusubi* and the top *mae-gashira* men against the grand champions. The result is, of course, that *komusubi* rankers almost inevitably get off to a bad start, end up with a mediocre record, and fall back again down the scale. An outstanding exception was Annenyama, who won the 1957 Summer Championship immediately after being promoted to *komusubi*.

It is estimated that only one wrestler in five hundred makes *ozeki*. *Ozeki* means "great barrier," which is precisely what it is. It's Sumo-dom's last great challenge. Less than half the *ozeki* make *yokozuna*, for a man has to have a number of first-class tournament perform-ances tucked in his belt before he's named grand champion.

There's one consolation, though. Once a *yokozuna*, always a *yokozuna*. A grand champion alone can never be demoted, how-ever poor his record. That would be much too undignified; and of all sports Sumo is the most dignified. It may, of course, be argued that the sacrosanct status of the *yokozuna* is thoroughly undemo-cratic, that there is something monarchical about the whole thing. Well, the grand champion, with all his regalia and all the cere-monial splendor that attends his entry on the stage is certainly very much like a king. He should not, many feel, be dethroned.

Promotion, incidentally, is not the only reward of which a suc-cessful wrestler may be proud. The winner of a tournament—the man with the best won-lost record—receives, after the bouts are over on the final day, the huge *shihai* or Emperor's Cup. This trophy is returned by the victor at a ceremony that takes place on the opening day of the following tournament and is replaced by a smaller replica which he may have for keeps. An interesting postwar innovation at each tournament has been the presentation, made by an American gentleman in formal Japanese attire and speaking impeccable Japanese, of a large trophy given by Pan American World Airways. Ancient and modern, cheek by jowl.

In addition to the Emperor's Cup for the winner, three consolation prizes, in the form of shields, are awarded at each tournament. They are the *shukun-sho,* or prize for outstanding achievement given to the grappler who upsets the most grand champions and champions; the *gino-sho,* or prize for skill, and the *kanto-sho* or prize for fighting spirit. Nor is that all. There is a well-known Japanese saying, *hana yori dango,* which roughly translated, means "I'd rather have dumplings than pretty flowers." Or, in other words, "appreciation should be shown in a more practical manner." So, previous to a bout, sometimes as many as seven or eight *yobi-dashi* or announcers walk around the ring each carrying a large banner. These bear the names of various companies which, for the sake of advertisement or, who knows, out of pure kindness of heart, wish to announce that they are awarding a prize to the winner of the bout.

The victor receives his prize from the referee as they both squat, but before actually taking it the wrestler makes three passes over it with his hand, first to the left, then to the right, and finally to the center. Black magic? Not at all. He is merely giving thanks to heaven, earth, and man in turn. No, the envelope does not contain currency or a check. It is simply a catalog from which he may

select whatever he happens to like.   But those seven or eight banners
may be worth seventy or eighty thousand yen in all to the winner.

A Typical Ranking List of the Leading Sumo Wrestlers

(Summer, 1957)

West			East		
Yokozuna	Kagamisato	(10-5)	*Yokozuna*	Tochinishiki	(12-3)
„	Yoshibayama	(5-6)	„	Chiyo-no-yama	(absent)
Ozeki	Asashio	(9-6)	*Ozeki*	Waka-no-hana	(11-4)
			„	Matsunobori	(8-7)
Sekiwake	Tokitsuyama	(11-4)	*Sekiwake*	Tama-no-umi	(0-6)
„	Wakahaguro	(7-8)			
Komusubi	Annenyama	(13-2)	*Komusubi*	Tsuru-ga-mine	(5-10)
„	Kotogahama	(12-3)			
Maegashira	1. Tochihikari	(5-10)	*Maegashira*	1. Ouchiyama	(7-8)
„	2. Naruyama	(2-13)	„	2. Dewanishiki	(6-9)
„	3. Wakamaeda	(5-10)	„	3. Kita-no-nada	(9-6)
„	4. Hoshikabuto	(5-10)	„	4. Shinobuyama	(6-9)
„	5. Narutoumi	(3-12)	„	5. Iwakaze	(4-11)
„	6. Shimizugawa	(10-5)	„	6. Mitsuneyama	(9-6)
„	7. Ohikari	(5-10)	„	7. Shimanishiki	(5-10)
„	8. Dewaminato	(0-2)	„	8. Tokinishiki	(10-5)
„	9. Wakasegawa	(7-8)	„	9. Futatsuryu	(8-7)
„	10. Araiwa	(8-7)	„	10. Daitenryu	(11-4)
„	11. Odachi	(8-7)	„	11. Osegawa	(7-8)
„	12. Wakabayama	(8-7)	„	12. Hajimayama	(8-7)

West continued:

Maegashira	13. Hirakagawa (absent)
"	14. Hirosegawa	(8–7)
"	15. Kuninobori	(8–7)
"	16. Yasome	(7–8)
"	17. Kiyoenami	(7–8)
"	18. O-no-ura	(8–7)
"	19. Izuminada	(8–7)
"	20. Fusanishiki	(11–4)
"	21. Yoshiiyama	(11–4)
"	22. Hiyodoshi	(5–10)

East continued:

Maegashira	13. Miyanishiki	(8–7)
"	14. Shionishiki	(8–7)
"	15. Takanishiki	(9–6)
"	16. Azumaumi	(5–10)
"	17. Yoshi-no-mine	(2–10)
"	18. Koi-no-se	(6–9)
"	19. Kamiyuyama	(6–9)
"	20. Kaminishiki	(7–8)
"	21. Fuku-no-umi	(8–7)
"	22. Orochigata	(4–11)
"	23. Mae-no-yama	(7–8)

(Figures in brackets show the wrestler's won-lost record in the summer tournament, 1957, the figure on the left indicating the number of matches won. *Komusubi* Annenyama, with a thirteen-two record was the winner. At times, due to sickness or injuries sustained during a bout, a wrestler is unable to continue until the end of the tournament. In the above record the won-lost scores that do not total fifteen represent such cases. It should be noted that the East and West men do not necessarily clash in the ring. The two classifications are for convenience' sake, half of the wrestlers coming down the east aisle and the other half down the west).

CHAPTER 6

"Psychological Warfare"

A Sumo wrestler's make-up consists of three parts. The first is physical, the second technical, and the third psychological. For the simple reason that a Sumo bout gets under way with psychological warfare, the latter merits prior discussion. It is, perhaps, the most difficult part of Sumo for a non-Oriental to appreciate.

Following an initial flexing of muscles and stamping of feet at the edge of the ring, the rivals pick up a handful of purifying salt, scatter it, and squat down facing each other at a respectful distance in the center of the arena. The referee keeps a watchful eye on them, meanwhile barking out words of encouragement and instruction. In the course of this ritual, which is known as the *shikiri-naoshi,* the contestants get down almost with their noses in the sand, pound the floor with their fists (Plate 2), and fix each other with piercing glances.

Like a grand champion's triumphal entry, to be described later, the *shikiri-naoshi* follows a set pattern. The whole thing, it should be noted, is limited to four minutes, during which period the rivals march back and forth between the center of the ring and "salt corner" about four or five times. When time is up, the time-keeper (one of the black-robed judges) nods to one of the young attendants sitting by the water pail. He in his turn stands up and nods to the contestants and to the referee.

For the *ju-ryo*—wrestlers ranking immediately below *maku-uchi* —the time allotted for *shikiri-naoshi* is only three minutes. And the very young wrestlers who perform in the early hours to empty benches don't go through the motions at all, but have to get on with their bout right away.

This basic element of Sumo, which very likely causes many Westerners to lose interest in the sport at the very outset and to mutter, "Why don't they cut out all that stuff?" is regarded as the very marrow of the art by those in the know and, indeed, by the wrestlers themselves. For it is during these seemingly grotesque posturings that the grapplers seek to read what is in each other's minds— to discover whether the other man appears likely to spring at once to the attack or to await his rival's onrush.

By taking a good peek at a wrestler's face as he makes his way each time to the center of the ring in the preliminaries, an expert observer can figure out whether or not he has a plan of campaign all nice and clear-cut in his head. He can tell when the man is still trying to make up his mind how to proceed and can distinguish a grappler who is brimful of confidence and quite composed from one who is all tense and jittery. It requires plenty of practice, of course, to spot all this. And if the observer is able to do it, you may be quite sure the wrestlers themselves can. Naturally, they aim to fool each other. A man who knows precisely what he is going to do, for instance, may trick the other fellow into thinking that he doesn't.

The second purpose of the *shikiri* is to give the wrestlers an opportunity gradually to work themselves up to the right pitch of excitement. In this sense, it may be termed a warming-up. It is the referee's job, by giving out a series of shrill, Kabuki-type ejaculations, to whip up the requisite amount of excitement in his charges.

The *shikiri-naoshi* is well worth more than a little study by the Sumo enthusiast. If he can muster sufficient interest in it he will no longer complain, as some people do, that Sumo is all froth and no beer.

The preliminaries over, the referee crouches down, gives the word, and the rivals spring toward each other. This is called the *tachi-ai* or the initial clash. It has been said that pitching is seventy-five per cent of baseball. Similarly, it might be said that the *tachi-ai* is seventy-five per cent of Sumo, for "thrice armed is he who gets his blow in first." A man who is late in the *tachi-ai* usually goes down to defeat, for the wrestler who is up first can, as a rule, direct the course of a bout as he pleases, putting his opponent on the defensive and often catching him off balance. There are, of course, exceptions. Some wrestlers are noted for staging wonderful recoveries after a bad *tachi-ai*, Grand Champion Tochinishiki, for instance. A bout may be won either by ejecting one's opponent from the ring or by downing him inside the arena. In the former case it spells defeat if so much as a toe is over the edge; in the latter a tilt is lost if any part of the body above (and including) the knee hits the dirt. And the winner may achieve his objective by any one of sixty-eight recognized techniques, known as *kimari-te*. The word is almost impossible to translate, for a man may be thrown, pushed, pulled, flipped, tapped, etc., either down or out.

There are, naturally, certain things that are taboo in Sumo. For

this is not all-in wrestling, by any means. It is forbidden to strike
a man with the fists. And the *karate* chop, a sledge-hammer whack
delivered with the side of the hand, popularized by the famous pro-
wrestler Rikidozan (an ex-Sumo man) is also prohibited. Hair-
pulling and eye-poking are frowned upon, as are slapping the ears
and grasping the throat. Not surprising, of course. Nor may a
wrestler kick his opponent in the belly or the chest. Nor yet in the
head. And, lastly, care must be exercised so as not to lay foul hands
on the *mae-tatemitsu*—that part of the grappler's attire that sweeps
down at right angles to the belly-band and covers the vital organs.
Violation of any one of the above embargoes would ensure automatic
defeat. It seldom occurs, however. The author himself, in the
course of many years of Sumo-viewing, only once saw the hair
pulled. No more than that.

CHAPTER 7

The Techniques of Sumo

Broadly speaking, it may be said that there are two types of Sumo—that in which the wrestlers come to grips and that in which they do not. A great number of true connoisseurs of the art will turn up their noses at the latter. They like the men to grapple. If they do, the bout is likely to last longer and provide more thrills. After all, the customer wants value for money.

By the end of the *shikiri-naoshi,* the preliminary posturing, the wrestler has—or should have—made up his mind whether he wishes to come to grips or not. Certain wrestlers invariably prefer not to do so. They like to slap their opponent toward the edge of the ring and then, when they've got him right off balance, push him out (see Plate 10). The leading modern exponent of this type of Sumo is Grand Champion Chiyo-no-yama (Plate 5). His strength lies in those long, powerful arms of his.

The slapping maneuver, which is known as *tsuppari,* although not so popular with the fans, is a most valuable weapon in a wrestler's armory. It enables him to polish off his man in double-quick time. A Sumo tournament lasts fifteen days and is an immense drain on a

6. GRAND CHAMPION TOCHINISHIKI: Tochinishiki goes through the ceremonial motions of the *dohyo-iri*. Behind him may be glimpsed the sword held by his *tachimochi* or swordbearer, standing on the edge of ring.

7. THE HEAVE-HO!: Grand Champion Tochinishiki (right) lifts his arch-rival, now Grand Champion Waka-no-hana, straight off the ground and hoists him bodily out of the ring. This type of heave-ho is known as *tsuri-dashi*. Note the intentness of the referee as he watches the rivals' feet.

9. AN UNUSUAL THROW: Quick as lightning, Champion Waka-no-hana (rear) deposits Toki-nishiki in the sand with a rare throw known as *yobi-modoshi*. He takes his opponent by the arm and simultaneously trips him. Waka-no-hana more or less has the monopoly of this throw.

8. UWATE-NAGE: The then champion Waka-no-hana sends Kita-no-nada sprawling with an *uwate-nage* or upper hand throw; i. e. the throw is achieved by Waka-no-hana's " upper " hand, the hand that is outside his opponent's hand.

10. Oshi-dashi: Grand champion Tochinishiki (right) is shown pushing Iwakaze out of the ring. This final push, or *oshi-dashi,* is preceded by a series of hearty slaps or *tsuppari* to drive the loser toward the edge of the arena.

fellow's physique. If, however, he can get through a bout in one second flat, which is about the absolute minimum, it's more or less equivalent to a day's rest. The average time required for a match is about 10 seconds; very few go on for over a minute. When they do, the customers roar and ask for more, but that's what really takes it out of a wrestler.

A further advantage of the slapping method is that there is less likelihood of leg injuries, the behemoths' biggest bugbear. Televiewers must have noticed the tremendous number of supporters adorning the knees, the weakest point of a sumoist. It is interesting to note that in recent tourneys Grand Champion Tochinishiki has taken a leaf out of stablemate Chiyo-no-yama's book and become a really proficient slapper. Slapping saves a lot of trouble for a man who has passed thirty.

For those who do not wish to grapple, slapping is not the only maneuver. There is, for example, *hataki-komi* which usually requires no more than a second to execute. What happens is that a man senses by the look in his opponent's eyes just before clinching that the latter is intent on getting the darned thing over quickly. So he simply steps to one side and gives his rival a hefty smack on the back as he flies past. Many a fan has been caught napping by a *hataki-komi*. It's all over in a jiffy.

Another quick maneuver is *ketaguri,* copyright held by the crafty Dewaminato. As his opponent rushes in, he kicks his legs from under him. Time required, one second. Then there's *ashi-tori,* for which Wakabayama holds the patent. He simply grabs his rival by the leg and has him hopping around the ring until he finally topples him over.

Now for the grappling types of Sumo, preferred by men like

11. Sumo throws. In Sumo there are numberless variations of throws, out of which, smaller groups of the recognized techniques have been evolved, these being the *kimari-te* and the *shijuhatte*. Here are some of those better known throws in use in the Sumo *dohyo* today. The wrestler wearing the black band represents the winner.

Maki-otoshi

Uwate-nage   Hatakikomi   Yorikiri   Ashi-tori

Nimaigeri   Shitate-dashinage   Uttchari   Shitate-yagura

Sotogake   Uchigake   Nodowa-zeme   Kubi-nage

Uwate-dashinage   Watashikomi   Kote-nage

Sukui-nage   Kirikaeshi   Katasukashi   Tsuri-dashi

Hiki-otoshi   Ketaguri   Tottari   Abise-taoshi

Amiuchi   Gyaku-hineri   Okuri-dashi   Uwate-yagura

Komatasukui   Sabaori   Shitate-nage   Koshi-nage

Oshi-dashi   Tsuki-otoshi   Tsuki-dashi

former grand champions Yoshibayama (see Plates 12 & 13) and
Kagamisato (Plate 14), who delight the genuine, dyed-in-the-wool
fan. In contrast to the lighter wrestlers, these fatties naturally prefer
to take the fullest advantage of their weight and to come to grips
with their opponent as soon as possible. For grappling purposes,
wrestlers may be divided into two categories, *hidari-yotsu,* or left-
handers, and *migi-yotsu,* or right-handers. The whole idea—and
this is what a televiewer should watch out for—is for the southpaw
to get his left or stronger arm inside the other man's right, and
conversely for the right-hander to thrust his right arm inside the
other's left. The man who can get his arms into a good position
before his opponent does so enjoys a very big advantage.

The next thing is to get a firm grip on the other's *mawashi* or
belly-band (see Plates 7, 17 & 18). The latter will try to prevent
this either by squirming about or by keeping the lower part of his
body at a very safe distance. The wily, long-bodied Koto-ga-hama
is a noted exponent of these maneuvers. His *mawashi* is always an
extremely difficult thing to grab hold of. There are also some
wrestlers who are open to criticism for repeatedly having their belly-
band loosely tied, so as not to afford their opponent a secure grip.
This, of course, is "not cricket." But a sharp referee will spot the
fact and quickly tighten things up.

Now comes the jockeying for position preparatory to the heave-ho.
With the immense, pot-bellied men the favorite tactic is gradually
to edge the opponent, using their tremendous weight, toward the
rim of the arena and gently march him out.   This tactic, known
as *yori-kiri* (see Plate 11), is the most common of all. A more thrilling variant is *yori-taoshi* (see Plate 16), in which victor and van-
quished go hurtling out of the ring together, with the former on

top. Timing, in this as in all Sumo moves, is of the utmost impor-
tance. A skillful wrestler bides his time until he can catch his rival
off balance and then launches his attack.

Wrestlers like the huge Champion Matsunobori (see Plate 19)
and ex-junior champion Tokitsuyama (see Plate 4) are fond of *tsuri-
dashi* (see Plate 7). They grasp their opponent's *mawashi* firmly
with both hands, then run him around till he's off balance and
finally hoist him high in the air and clean out of the ring. This
is something truly Herculean. Then there's the miraculous *uttchari*
(see Plate 3). This occurs when a man, on the point of being
toppled out, digs in on the edge of the ring, hoists his rival up over
his stomach and, with a quick turn, flings him out, himself following
a tenth of a second later.

Coming now to tactics aimed at dumping a man inside the ring,
it can be noted that some wrestlers are adept at using their legs to
trip an opponent. One such is Koto-ga-hama, employing his favorite
uchi-gake (see Plate 18). Choosing his moment to a nicety, he will
suddenly thrust a limb between his rival's legs and upset him with
a neat trip. Others favor the *soto-gake,* in which a leg is wound
outside the opponent's—with the same result.

The beautiful *uwate-nage* (see Plate 8) and *shitate-nage* are throws
by which lighter men, such as Grand Champion Waka-no-hana,
often overthrow much heavier opponents. The former may be
translated the "upper-hand throw," the latter the "under-hand
throw." The "upper" refers to the hand that is outside the other
man's arm, the "under" to that which is inside it. In the *uwate-
nage* the throw is executed with the outside hand, in the *shitate-nage*
with the inside hand. More often than not quite a lot of maneuver-
ing takes place and several fruitless attempts are made at a throw

before an opponent is finally caught off balance and flung down.

The above description includes some of the throws most commonly seen. But there are countless variations, depending on exactly how a man is thrown, pulled, pushed, slapped, kicked, and so on, either down or out. To describe them all would require a volume in itself.

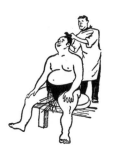

CHAPTER 8

Grand Champions

There are three grand champions in the Year of Grace, 1958. The number is by no means arbitrary. There have been two only in the past; there may be two again. Or, again, there may even be as many as five; there's nothing in the rules of Sumo to prevent it.

The senior grand champion is the tremendously tall, giant spider-like Chiyo-no-yama (Plate 5), who was born in Hokkaido in 1926, the son of a fisherman-farmer. He was a stand-out even as a youth and was told by a prowling news-hawk that he would go far if he would only step up to the capital and place his feet on the first rung of the Sumo ladder.

In 1942, the year following the outbreak of the Pacific War, Chiyo-no-yama enrolled in the large gym run by Dewa-no-umi, ex-grand champion Tsune-no-hana, the tragic figure who, weighed down by the heavy burden of responsibility thrown onto his shoulders as head of the Japan Sumo Association at a critical stage in its history in 1957, attempted suicide. Chiyo-no-yama's progress was rapid. As early as the fall of 1949 he was already *ozeki* and had grabbed his first tourney championship. He followed up this initial triumph with a second victory in the very next tournament (spring, 1950).

One would, perhaps, have imagined that his successive triumphs would at once have secured him promotion to the coveted rank of *yokozuna*. The council of selectors, however, who meet to discuss questions of elevation and demotion after each tourney, are hard men to please. The tall youngster had to wait until the year 1951, when he gathered in the trophy with a magnificent record of fourteen wins and one defeat, for his reward. After his great success in the summer tournament of that year he was finally, when still only twenty-five years of age, created grand champion.

And then something happened. For some unexplainable reason he began to slip. Tournament followed tournament as he saw his rivals repeatedly snatch the prize from his grasp. The sensitive Chiyo-no-yama was in the end driven to suggesting that he abdicate, forfeit his crown, and start from the bottom again. Such a thing had never occurred before. Grand champions are never demoted; they just carry on until they are old enough to retire. It was preposterous. Chiyo-no-yama was persuaded to reconsider his decision. He did so, and finally, after twelve tourneys without a grain of comfort, his name was in the spotlight again when he captured the New Year's championship of 1955 for his fourth triumph.

The big man's revival was consolidated by a victory in the following tourney, at Osaka in the spring. Then again there was an interval of six meets without a win, but the "Big Spider" registered his sixth and latest success at New Year's, 1957. With six successes in all to his credit, Chiyo-no-yama is surpassed only by Grand Champion Tochinishiki.

The second grand champion, Tochinishiki (see Plates 6 & 10) is often known as *meijin,* or the master-craftsman. Unlike his two colleagues, he is a city man. The son of an umbrella-maker, he was born and brought up in Tokyo. With all the rain Japan gets one would think umbrella-making should be a profitable business. History, however, does not record that the *meijin's* father amassed a fortune.

A year younger than his friend Chiyo-no-yama—the two belong to the same group of gyms and so never clash in the ring—Tochinishiki relies on skill as much as on weight to down his opponents. He is a mere (?) 250 pounds, in contrast to ex-grand champions Kagamisato's and Yoshibayama's 320. His speed is phenomenal; he is a master of strategy, and he can vary his tactics to suit the occasion or his opponent. The phrase "brains rather than brawn" may well be applied to this master wrestler. He has, however, put on quite a lot of weight since being named grand champion and is beginning to develop a "pot."

On his way to the top Tochinishiki was awarded the *gino-sho*, the prize for the most skillful wrestler, nine times, a record. But something more than skill is needed if such a comparatively small man is to scale the heights. And Tochinishiki has it in a high degree. That something is just plain guts. Here is a man who will never admit defeat. Many a time in the course of a long, drawn-out bout he seems to be a goner. Then, as if by a miracle, he turns the tables on his opponent and emerges triumphant. A case in point was the tilt on the last day of the summer tournament of 1955, a tournament won by Tochinishiki. On this occasion the usually lethargic, huge Ouchiyama suddenly came to life, giving Tochi the shock of his life. Taken by surprise, the grand champion made a bad start but hung on grimly. Finally, with an almost superhuman effort, he threw his rival by the neck, using the throw known as *kubi-nage.*

Tochinishiki has a record of seven championships gained in all. The first was in the fall tourney of 1952, when he was still *sekiwake*, and the second in the spring of the following year, by which time he was *ozeki*. Successive triumphs followed in the summer and autumn of 1954, resulting in his elevation to grand champion. Three tourneys later came his fifth victory, in the summer of 1955, after a two-year interval, his sixth in the autumn of 1957, and seventh in the summer of 1958.

The youngest and latest grand champion, Waka-no-hana (see Plates 7, 8 & 9), is by far the most popular of the three. In fact, it would scarcely be going too far to say that he is the most popular figure in the whole of Japanese sport.

He first saw the light of day in 1928 in Aomori, the prefecture at the extreme northern end of Honshu, the main island, a prefecture that has produced any number of fine sumoists, including the paunchy ex-grand champion Kagamisato, who retired at the close of the New Year's tournament of 1958.

It was in 1946, the year after the termination of the war, that Waka-no-hana, then a callow youth of eighteen, came down from the north to try his fortune in the Sumo ring. He entered the Nisho-no-seki gym, graced in pre-war days by the illustrious Grand Champion Tamanishiki.

At first he found the going rough, so rough in fact that he grew despondent of ever making out and actually contemplated suicide as a way out. It is recorded that the noted Rikidozan, now a grunt-and-groaner but then Waka-no-hana's senior in Nisho-no-seki, was instrumental in smacking the nonsense out of the lad. They are now the closest of friends.

Waka later transferred to the Hanakago gym in the same group.

He grew in strength and skill and finally got as high as *ozeki* at New Year's, 1956. In the summer of the same year he won his first championship.

It was a most eventful year for him, a year full of joys and sorrows. He lost his only son, a child of four, who was scalded to death when he overturned a steaming pot of *chanko-nabe*, wrestler's stew. Then, in the autumn, when he was riding high with eleven wins and no defeats and threatening to repeat his summer's success and assure himself of promotion to *yokozuna,* he was suddenly taken ill and was hospitalized.

Thereafter, at every tournament, he developed a habit of sweeping all before him for ten days or so and then collapsing like a pricked balloon. It began to seem that the highest honor in Sumo-dom would elude him. The people were for him, he was their hero, who had appeared personally in the movie, The Waka-no-hana Story. They waited anxiously for him to come through.

And then, in one of the most sensational tournaments of recent years, he did come through, at New Year's, 1958. Grand Champion Yoshibayama, with a poor record, announced his retirement midway through the tourney, and Grand Champion Kagamisato at the end of it. Amid all the excitement, Waka-no-hana slipped in, won his second championship and became the 45th *yokozuna.*

Some Ex-Greats

The records of the currently active grand champions, however, almost pale into insignificance when compared with the stupendous achievements of Futabayama (the present Tokitsukaze), who has no less than twelve triumphs to his name. This magnificent wrestler notched his first in the summer of 1936 as a *sekiwake,* or junior champion, and then proceeded to take the next four in a row (the first two when he was champion). And what is even more remarkable is that he went through the entire five tournaments without once going down to defeat. Futabayama, whose final triumph came in the war year of 1943, actually fought at one period as many as sixty-nine bouts without a single loss, a feat without parallel in the long history of Sumo. In the seventieth bout the grand champion was finally toppled by *sekiwake* (later *yokozuna*) Aki-no-umi.

Other outstanding records were those of Tachiyama (nine championships) at the end of the Meiji and the beginning of the Taisho eras (1910-1916) and of Tochigiyama (the present Kasugano, master of the gym to which Tochnishiki belongs), who racked up nine championships in the Taisho era between 1917 and 1925. Tsune-no-hana (later Dewa-no-umi) was another great performer, who ran out victorious ten times between the years 1923 and 1930, embracing both the Taisho and Showa eras. Tamanishiki, whose death, due to appendicitis, in 1938 at the early age of thirty-five came as a staggering blow to Sumo-dom, triumphed seven times between 1931 and 1936.

In more recent times, following the retirement of the great Futabayama, Haguroyama (the present Tatsunami) took six championships, starting in 1944 and winding up in 1952. Another colorful figure was Grand Champion Azumafuji, who emerged on the winning side in six tournaments. This 370-pounder, whose last triumph was in the fall of 1953, withdrew from Sumo circles because of dissatisfaction over the then-prevailing feudalistic conditions and

joined the ranks of the "grunt 'n groan" pro-wrestlers. He followed
the noted Rikidozan, who reached *sekiwake* rank before seceding.
There can be little doubt that the secessions of Rikidozan and
Azumafuji, together with that of lesser lights, was the first step in
the de-feudalization of the ancient sport.

Complete List of Grand Champions

1st.	Akashi	17th century
2nd.	Maruyama	1712–1749
3rd.	Ayagawa	1700– ?
4th.	Tanikaze	1750–1795
5th.	Onogawa	1758–1805
6th.	Ao-no-matsu	1791–1851
7th.	Inazuma	1795–1877
8th.	Shiranui I	1801–1854
9th.	Hide-no-yama	1808–1862
10th.	Unryu	1823–1891
11th.	Shiranui II	1825–1879
12th.	Jimmaku	1829–1903
13th.	Kimenzan	1826–1871
14th.	Sakaigawa	1843–1889
15th.	Ume-ga-tani I	1845–1928
16th.	Nishi-no-umi I	1855–1908
17th.	Konishiki	1867–1914
18th.	Ozutsu	1870–1918
19th.	Hitachiyama	1874–1922
20th.	Ume-ga-tani II	1878–1927

List of Grand Champions continued:

21st.	Wakashima	1876–1943
22nd.	Tachiyama	1877–1941
23rd.	Okido	1877–1916
24th.	Otori	1887–
25th.	Nishi-no-umi II	1880–1931
26th.	Onishiki I	1855–1908
27th.	Tochigiyama	1892–
28th.	Onishiki II	1891–1941
29th.	Miyagiyama	1895–1943
30th.	Nishi-no-umi III	1890–1933
31st.	Tsune-no-hana	1896–
32nd.	Tamanishiki	1903–1938
33rd.	Musashiyama	1909–
34th.	Minanogawa	1903–
35th.	Futabayama	1912–
36th.	Haguroyama	1914–
37th.	Aki-no-umi	1914–
38th.	Terukuni	1919–
39th.	Maedayama	1914–
40th.	Azumafuji	1921–
41st.	Chiyo-no-yama	1926–
42nd.	Kagamisato	1922–
43rd.	Yoshibayama	1920–
44th.	Tochinishiki	1925–
45th.	Waka-no-hana	1928–

(Note: The twenty-seventh grand champion, Tochigiyama (under the name of Kasugano); the thirty-first, Tsune-no-hana (Dewa-no-umi); the thirty-fifth, Futabayama (Tokitsukaze); the thirty-sixth,

Haguroyama (Tatsunami); the thirty-eighth, Terukuni (Araiso) and the thirty-ninth, Maedayama (Takasago), all operate Sumo gyms for the training of wrestlers.)

CHAPTER 9

Pageantry

Pageantry and ceremony invariably play a prominent role in the life of countries like Japan and Britain with a long history and tradition.

Possibly nowhere else in the world do colorful festivals abound in every corner of the land as they do in Japan. The great medieval processions that take place annually in Kyoto and Nikko are but two examples. Then there is Kabuki with all its gorgeous color. And Sumo is no exception. It is crammed full of pageantry. This is only natural when one considers Sumo's original tie-up with religion—the first tournament was held in the grounds of a temple—and also the fact that the wrestlers regularly performed at court and before the great daimyo, or feudal lords, and other dignitaries.

It may be no exaggeration to say that, in all sport, there is no more brilliant spectacle than the triumphal entry of the grand champions. Termed the *dohyo-iri,* this takes place every day of each fifteen-day tournament. Around three-thirty in the afternoon when the minor

12. YORI-KIRI: Ex-Grand Champion Yoshibayama (right) by main strength forces his opponent Wakahaguro out of the ring. In *yori-kiri* both wrestlers usually finish up on their feet. It is the gentlest way of winning.

13. Ex-Grand Champion Yoshibayama: Yoshibayama crouches and extends his palms at the *dohyo-iri*. In the rear at left is the referee. Note the huge knot (behind) of the grand champion's *tsuna*.

14. Ex-Grand Champion Kagamisato: Wearing the traditional *tsuna* or hawser, Shinto-style paper streamers and ceremonial apron, Kagamisato is about to clap his hands, one of the conventional features of the *dohyo-iri*.

bouts, which have been going on since early morning, have been safely tucked away, the *yobidashi,* or announcer, steps into the arena and beats his clappers, the ring is carefully swept, and one half of the top-ranking *maku-uchi* wrestlers stride in Indian file down the aisle leading to the ring. They are clad in beautifully embroidered *kesho-mawashi* (see Plates 5, 6, 12, 13, 14 & 20), aprons of multi-colored brocade, of every design you can imagine. If your eyes are sharp enough and you can read the Japanese writing on them, you can no doubt make out the wrestler's name.

How on earth, you may wonder, can they afford such magnificent apparel? The answer is, they can't. The aprons are, in nine cases out of ten, given by patrons. Every self-respecting wrestler has his patron—and very often his patroness as well. A good-quality apron will run up to as much as ¥300,000 (or about $800); and they say some wrestlers have so many of them they can wear a different one each day of the tournament and then have some left over.

The wrestlers, about twenty in all, next step up into the ring and form a circle round it, clap their hands in unison, go through an amusing little routine in which they saucily hitch up their aprons half an inch or so, and then withdraw by the same route as they came. The remaining half of the top-rankers then march down the opposite aisle and go through identical motions in the arena. This impressive spectacle might well be called the "Grand March of the Gladiators"

Now comes the *piece de résistance,* the ceremonial entry of the grand champions. Amid thunderous applause from the fans, a superbly gowned little *gyoji* (see Plates 5, 7, 13 & 15), or referee—of whom more anon—follows a clapper-beating announcer down the aisle. Next comes the grand champion's *tsuyuharai*, or attendant. Then the great man himself and finally, bringing up the rear, his *tachimochi*, or sword-bearer.

Before they hoist themselves into the arena, let us glance at one of the great men's apparel. Most striking is the massive rope or hawser that encircles him below his magnificently jutting stomach (see Plates 5, 6, 13, 14, 15 & 16). The handiwork of the young wrestlers who wait on him hand and foot, it appears to weigh anything up to sixteen tons. It is tied at the back in a picturesque bow. From this rope *(tsuna)* is derived the name *yokozuna* (meaning "side rope"). It is the symbol of his lofty status. The white zig-zag *gohei,* or paper streamers, hanging from the rope afford evidence of Sumo's religious associations; they are identical with those seen at the entrance to a Shinto shrine. The grand champion's fancy apron is, of course, even more gorgeous than those of the lesser lights.

Spear-headed by the diminutive referee, all four participants in the ceremony step up into the ring. The great man, flanked by his retainers, squats down and then, after rising and bowing to the gallery, marches like the monarch he is to the center of the arena. Then comes the moment all the thousands of children in the audience have been waiting for hour upon hour. As he balances himself on one leg and brings the other down with a loud thump to the ground, the youngsters set up a roar of approval that threatens to raise the roof.

The motions the grand champion goes through may be split up into three classifications—the clapping of the hands, the extending of the arms, and the stamping of the feet. They follow a fixed form and there can be no ad-libbing. Actually, there are two styles, known as the *unryu* (originated in the nineteenth century by Unryu, tenth *yokozuna*) and the *shiranui* (first performed by Shiranui, eighth *yokozuna*). The present-day grand champions, Chiyo-no-yama, Tochinishiki, and Waka-no-hana follow the *unryu* style. What's the difference? Well, the *unryu* is described as being "defensive" and the *shiranui*—it might give offense to call it "offensive"— "aggressive."

Going back to religion (or is it superstition?) again, the clapping of the hands is said to be for the purpose of attracting the attention of the gods. A Japanese does this habitually when he pays a visit to a shrine. The extending of the arms and the turning up of the palms is to show, symbolically, that the wrestler has no weapon concealed. In other words, he is pure and will fight clean. And the stamping of the feet symbolizes the stamping of everything that is evil into the ground.

All this done, the grand champion retires to the edge of the ring, bows once more, and withdraws, his place to be taken by the remaining grand champions in turn. When all have gone through the ritual the announcer again beats his clappers to attract the gods' attention and the breath-taking spectacle is over.

Bow Ceremony

An interesting little *yumitori-shiki,* or bow-twirling ceremony follows the concluding bout each day (see Plate 21). It appears at first glance to have little to do with Sumo. Its history is as follows: In the third year of the Tensho era (1575) the great warrior-lord, Oda Nobunaga, to celebrate his victory in battle, held a great Sumo tournament at Azuchi Castle, in what is now known as Shiga

Prefecture. Notices went out all over the country to the effect that the winning wrestler would be given the colossal prize of five hundred *koku* (1 *koku* equals 4.96 bushels) of rice, for in those days everything was reckoned in terms of *koku*. One Ganzaemon won the tourney and, in addition to the rice, was presented by the great lord with a bow, the very same bow, it is claimed, that is used in the ceremony today. And to commemorate this historic occasion the winner of each tournament was given the privilege of performing the *yumitori-shiki* after the final bout on the last day.

A change was made in 1952, and the show is now given daily by a hand-picked wrestler, Otayama, who has made the bow routine his special line. The *yumitori-shiki* may be said to round off the day's proceedings nicely.

CHAPTER 10

The Referee

It may be considered strange that a mere referee should grab a whole chapter for himself. Yet it is no more than the Sumo arbiter deserves. He is unique (see Plates 2, 4, 5, 7, 12 & 14).

To conjure up a vision of this colorful character one must first of all obliterate all pre-conceived ideas of what a referee or umpire should be and jettison all one's Occidental notions. Take, for example, the referee in soccer. Theoretically, he is supposed to efface himself while at the same time maintaining control of the game. He is not a part of the spectacle at all. That is to say, not until he brings down on his head the wrath of the fans by giving a decision against the home team; then, of course, he holds the center of the stage with all the spotlights turned on.

The "men in the blue suits" who officiate in baseball are somewhat more conspicuous than their soccer counterparts but the common view is to regard them in the light of a necessary evil. In both cases they are more often the object of derision and abuse than of respect. In the worst event they may even become the target of a barrage of rotten fruit, eggs, or other missiles.

The referee in Sumo, on the other hand, is regarded with supreme respect. There are lots of what might be termed close plays. But, however he may call them—and like baseball's great Bill Klem, he calls 'em as he sees 'em—his decision is never challenged by the fans; nor by the wrestlers themselves. There is no booing, no catcalls if a popular wrestler is not declared the winner. And the unfortunate loser does not argue or with venom flashing in his eyes shake his fist in the arbiter's face. It is simply not done. He retires, gracefully, to the showers. The ring is considered sacrosanct, so that anything in the nature of a barrage of fruit, vegetables, or dairy products would be looked upon as an outrage, and the offender—if such an extremely improbable event ever occurred—lynched by the crowd or sentenced to six months in the penitentiary.

Sumo referees, known as *gyoji,* are all given the family name either of Kimura or Shikimori. This is the tradition which has been followed from time immemorial. They start out at the tender age of thirteen or fourteen by officiating at the bouts held between the teen-age novices very early in the morning. Then, their work over, they go to school like any other kid.

The referees, like the grapplers themselves, have a ranking. And they dress according to their rank, very simply in the lower grades, then gradually ascending in gorgeousness until at the top they are a blaze of color. Look at the tassel on the fans they carry. It will provide a clue to their rank. Imperial purple (for the *tate-gyoji,* or referee-in-chief, only) is the highest, followed by purple and white, maroon, red and white, blue and white, and blue, right down to funereal black, the lowest. The youngest referees officiate barefoot. Their seniors wear white *tabi,* or socks, and sandals.

A senior referee in all his brocaded splendor is always very much in the Sumo picture. For instance, he heads the triumphal march of the grand champions down the aisle preparatory to their daily *dohyo-iri* ritual, at which he is anything but a mere bit player. And, he is not only seen, but very much heard. Following the *dohyo-iri* it is his duty to read out from large sheets of paper, which he displays to each side of the ring in turn, the following day's main bouts. The names of the wrestlers, written by himself with a brush in large Chinese characters, are called out in the peculiar high-pitched tones of a Kabuki actor. It has to be heard to be believed. The style is traditional and has at least the virtue of penetrating to every nook and corner of the vast amphitheater.

In the wake of the announcer, the referee also calls out the names of the wrestlers who are to clash in the next bout. Then they step up into the ring and, as they go through their four minutes of *shikiri-naoshi,* he bawls out something to work up their excitement and finally instructs them that "time is up" and that they had better "git rasslin'." The wrestlers know when time is up, not only because the referee barks "Time!" but because they are also apprised of the fact by a young fellow who jumps up for this purpose behind the place where the purifying salt is kept. "But how is the audience to know?" It's quite simple. All they have to do is to keep their eyes on the referee and his fan. When he squats right down and the fan, which previously has been facing sideways, faces them—if they are televiewing, that is—that means the equivalent of "play ball!"

A referee takes charge of bouts featuring wrestlers holding a rank corresponding to his own, and only the top man himself is entitled to handle the very last tilt of the day, in which one of the two rivals is always a grand champion. He takes charge of about three matches before being replaced by a colleague. A referee is only human, of course and, like even the best of politicians, sometimes makes a mistake. If he makes two, however, he is demoted and steps down the ladder a rung.

Mention was made earlier of the teen-age referees who brandish their fans some time before the sun is up. At the other end of the scale is the venerable Shikimori I-no-suke, of the shrill voice and white goatee, who is over seventy. Fifty-five years a referee; that's his record, one that will be very hard to beat.

Questions of salary are always interesting. I-no-suke, who ranks second, and the senior referee, Kimura Sho-no-suke, each haul in a total of seventy thousand yen a month. Referees corresponding in rank to *san-yaku* wrestlers get forty-five thousand and those corresponding to *maku-uchi* men, thirty thousand. Plus special allowances for each tournament.

CHAPTER 11

The Honorable Judges

Anyone who has ever sat through a Sumo tournament will doubtless agree that there are times when it would take the wisdom of a Solomon to decide the winner of a bout.

Two gigantic bodies take off more or less simultaneously from the arena, hurtle through space, and land with a thud somewhere in the vicinity of the front row of spectators. Question—who went out first? It happens on occasion that one behemoth is flung beautifully out of the ring while his opponent remains inside it, apparently a certain winner. But no, before sending his rival seemingly to his doom, he has stepped an eighth of an inch outside the arena and is thus the loser. The referee really has to keep his eyes skinned so as not to miss these fine points. But "to err is human" and, as was pointed out in the previous chapter, miss he sometimes does.

To ensure, therefore, that justice prevails and the palm is awarded to the right man, Sumo has its court of appeals. Seated at intervals around the ring are five *kensa-yaku,* or judges. Clad in the traditional ceremonial attire of the *haori,* a loose black robe flopping over the *hakama,* a thicker black skirt. The *haori* bears the family crest.

Should the referee be in doubt and appeal to the panel or should he err in his decision with a resulting protest from one or more of the judges, there follows what is known as a *mono-ii,* or pow-wow. When this occurs, the five judges hoist themselves out of their seats and into the ring and thrash out the moot point, complete with gesticulations to indicate what they think has taken place. The referee himself plays no part in these deliberations. He awaits, at times no doubt in fearful trepidation, the outcome.

As often as not, the other members of the panel accept the view of the judge who chanced to be seated nearest the spot where the wrestlers were at the crucial moment. But not necessarily so; and if the thing was so close that no agreement can be reached on the winner, a *tori-naoshi* takes place. This means that the bout must be fought all over again. A decision to stage a *tori-naoshi* is invariably greeted, for obvious reasons, with prolonged applause by the cash customers. They like to get a bit more for their money.

Should no decision be reached even after this second installment, the bout is re-staged following two intervening tilts and a chance given the by-this-time-exhausted gladiators to regain their energies in the dressing-room. And, if even after that one man finds it impossible to win and the other to lose, the judges wash their hands of the whole thing and call it a day and a draw. But this very rarely happens. Incidentally, until the summer of 1957 there used to be a *kensa-cho,* a sort of Lord Chief Justice, to whom a final appeal would be made. But with the recent democratization of the sport, this office was thought to be too autocratic and has been thrown to the winds.

One of the judges acts as timekeeper. A timekeeper is indispensable, not only to determine when the wrestlers shall get down to work but also decide when a bout shall be temporarily halted in the event of no decision being reached. For naturally they cannot go on puffing and blowing at each other endlessly, all to no avail. They have, as it were, to come up for air. The timekeeper motions to the referee and the rivals depart to their respective corners to have their belly-bands tightened, to wipe off the sweat, and to slake their thirst with water.

Now a word or two as to the identity of the judges and the method of their appointment. As might be expected, they are all former wrestlers of at least *maku-uchi* rank, but not necessarily all ex-grand champions or ex-champions, for the best wrestlers do not always make the best judges. Many of them are masters of the gyms where the wrestlers do their training. What's that about favoritism? No dice—there are too many judges; favoritism is out of the question.

A total of twelve judges are selected each New Year—though there is nothing arbitrary about this number. They bear different names from those they had in the days when they were active in the ring. For instance Futabayama, Sumo's greatest modern wrestler, who once went through sixty-nine bouts without a defeat, now calls himself Tokitsukaze. Tokitsukaze is a busy man. In addition to his duties as a judge, he runs his own gym, and is also president of the Japan Sumo Association.

The reader may be wondering whether there are any teen-age judges, just as there are teen-age wrestlers and teen-age referees in the early tilts. The answer to that one is that there are none. This is one job where age definitely gets the nod. In the early morning encounters, however, the number of judges is limited to two, one on the east side of the ring, the other on the west.

The honorable judges, by the way, are paid for their work just like anybody else. They are honorable, but not honorary, judges.

CHAPTER 12

So Clean and Gentlemanly

"Cleanliness," runs an old saying, " is next to godliness." It certainly is in Sumo, at any rate. Make no mistake about that.

Originally, Sumo may be said to have been a form of entertainment offered to the gods. Indeed, as we have seen, the first tournament ever was held in a temple compound. The grand champions, it has been noted, have white zig-zag *gohei* hanging from the rope that encircles their waist. The same type of thing may be seen at the entrance to a Shinto shrine. To call the attention of the gods, it is believed, wooden clappers are beaten by the announcer before the ceremony of the *dohyo-iri* and also prior to the concluding bout of the day. So much for the godliness.

The cleanliness follows as naturally as night follows day. To take, first of all, the scattering of salt in the ring by the wrestlers that plays such a prominent part in the pre-bout proceedings. A whole bale of it, they say, is used up in a couple of days, and one can well believe it. Quite mystifying to the Westerner, this ritual. Religious in origin, of course, its object is the purification of the ring. It can well be imagined that if a wrestler should ever forget to do his salt-scattering he would consider that his luck was out and that he would inevitably lose his match. It is interesting to note the various styles of salt-scattering. Some wrestlers fling it down in a more or less perfunctory manner, almost contemptuously, in fact. Others, among whom Annenyama, the great young hopeful, is an outstanding example, throw it joyously high in the air.

So much for the salt. Now to turn to the water. Yes, that's all it is, although some spectators may be running away with the false idea that it's something stronger than just Adam's ale the grapplers take at the ringside before and after a contest. The wrestlers don't drink the water. They merely rinse their mouths and immediately spit it out; for, like the salt routine, this water business is nothing more than a purification rite. Two large pails are kept in opposite corners of the ring; out of them the water is ladled with wooden dippers. The rinsing of the mouth is a must. And certain wrestlers, it should be added, are even more particular. They meticulously and ostentatiously wipe underneath the armpits with tissue paper, to remove any offensive perspiration. This takes place, curiously enough, before a bout, not after; the idea is to start out clean and pure.

To return to the ring. In addition to the thorough salting it undergoes from morning to evening, it is carefully swept and smoothed down at frequent intervals. Any piece of foreign matter is tossed out, often by the wrestlers themselves. From time to time, the arena is also given a sprinkling of water. But it is on the somewhat infrequent occasions when blood is drawn, quite accidentally of course, and spills on the floor of the arena that one realizes what tremendous stress is laid in the world of Sumo on purification. With so much slapping going on it is natural that a nose, for instance, should bleed from time to time. And, should any of the blood fall and defile the sacred ring, the contestants at once withdraw until the mess has been cleaned up. This is no simple matter, either. The foul section is scraped and scraped again, swept and smoothed over and over and then inspected until no doubt at all remains that everything is in order and the bout may be resumed.

It is in no sense of carping criticism that it has to be noted that, unfortunately, the ideal of cleanliness does not extend as far as the auditorium.

Now for another feature of Sumo that is to be found in very few other sports, or at any rate to the same degree. Reference is made to its gentlemanly character. In this respect it resembles particularly the typically British sports of rugby football and cricket. It is considered extremely bad form to question in any way a decision made by the referee in the former game or by the umpire in the latter. As previously mentioned in the chapter titled "The Referee" the same remark may be applied to Sumo.

It is a well-known Oriental trait not to betray one's inner feelings —hence references to the so-called "Oriental mask." And this trait is nowhere more in evidence than in the Sumo ring. The wrestlers are seldom stirred to anger—foul tactics are extremely rare—but even if they were so stirred, the spectators would never be aware of it. In Sumo a display of temper, such as may be seen on the soccer field or the baseball diamond, is unthinkable. Undoubtedly the religious angle has very much to do with it, Sumo being just as much a rite as it is a sport.

Imagine a soccer player or a professional wrestler helping an opponent up from the ground after he has felled him! Yet that is exactly what happens in Sumo, where the helping hand is invariably extended to a fallen rival. Again, after stepping up into the ring for his match, a wrestler is handed a dipperful of water by the winner of the previous tilt. That is the gentlemanly thing for a winner to do, rather than making an unseemly dash for the showers. Actually, it's a steaming hot bath he enjoys after his labors.

It is also regarded as good etiquette for a wrestler to bow in the direction of the ring on his arrival from the dressing-room and to do likewise prior to his return. Just another indication of the shrine-like atmosphere that surrounds the ring. The same custom is still observed at certain girls' high schools in Japan. On reaching the school gates as they are leaving to return home the girls turn around and bow to the school as a gesture of respect.

Sumo Nomenclature

The nomenclature of Sumo, in common with many aspects of the sport, is something out of this world.

The ordinary Tom, Dick, or Harriet in Japan has the suffix *san* tacked on to his or her name, corresponding to our Mr., Mrs. or Miss. Not so with the wrestlers, at least in their professional capacity. They are labeled *seki,* Chiyo-no-yama (Plate 5), for instance, being referred to as Chiyo-no-yama-seki (pronounced *zeki*). Also, a wrestler in the course of his career bears at least three names, and sometimes more, for a man may decide on a change in the belief that thereby he may win the favor of Lady Luck. For, like stage folk, the big grapplers are extremely superstitious.

To take the case of the greatest wrestler of the age, the peerless Futabayama (Plate 1). He was born, way down south in Oita Prefecture (Kyushu), Sadaji Akiyoshi. Then, for his Sumo monicker, he took the name of his patron, Futaba, and added the suffix *yama* or mountain. (No, Futaba is not Scotch for football; it means "two leaves.") Finally, when he retired from active competition and set up a *heya,* or gym, of his own, his name became Tokitsukaze

15. GRAND CHAMPION WAKA-NO-HANA: Newly promoted Grand Champion Waka-no-hana, flanked by his attendants performing the *dohyo-iri,* a ceremony reserved for grand champions only.

16. AFTER THE DAY'S BOUT: The new grand champion, Waka-no-hana and friends.

17. YORI-TAOSHI: In *yori-taoshi* both wrestlers go head-long out of the ring, the man on top being the winner. Here Hirosegawa is seen toppling Takanishiki.

18. UCHI-GAKE: Koto-ga-hama (on top) uses his favorite *uchi-gake* throw to defeat Iwakaze. In this throw Koto-ga-hama has inserted his left leg between the legs of his opponent and then toppled him over.

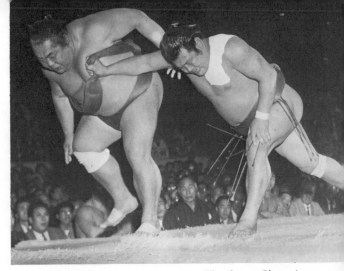

19. A MAMMOTH OUSTED: The huge Champion
Matsunobori (left) is pushed out of the arena by
Koto-ga-hama, who has taken firm hold of his
rival's belly-band. Note Koto-ga-hama's heavily-
bandaged left shoulder.

20. SUKUI-NAGE: In this throw Wakabayama
(right) swings Naruyama neatly round and then
deposits him on the floor.

21 YUMITORI-SHIKI: Otayama is here performing the *yumi-tori-shiki* or bow ceremony, which is held at the conclusion of each day's bouts at a grand tournament.

(*kaze*—pronounced "kazay"—means "wind"). This second name-change occurs when a wrestler quits the ring and his topknot is shorn off by the master of his gym.

Certain suffixes constantly recur in Sumo nomenclature, the most common being *yama* and *gawa*. For a giant wrestler nothing could be more apt than to stick *yama* on to the end of his name. And *gawa* or river is surely appropriate in that after many windings and tribulations it finally reaches its goal; the wrestler's goal is the rank of *yokozuna*. *Umi*, found in a number of names, means "the sea"; as with *yama*, its very size makes it fitting for use in Sumo. *Shio*, too, is common, meaning "tide." It may be said to denote the ebb and flow of a wrestler's fortunes in the arena. The name Asashio means "morning tide."

One often comes across the suffix *nishiki* after a name. It means "brocade" and is derived from the gorgeous ceremonial brocade aprons the wrestlers wear when they stage their daily parade around the arena. Prominent *nishiki*-tagged men are Grand Champion Tochinishiki (see Plate 3 & 11), and also Shionishiki, Tokinishiki and Miyanishiki. *Nobori*, as in Matsunobori (see Plate 18), means "ascent," symbolizing the climb up the Sumo ladder of success. *Ryu*, seen in Futatsuryu and Daitenryu, is "dragon," calculated to strike fear into the heart of a rival.

So much for the suffixes most frequently found in Sumo-dom. Now for the fore portion of the names, which sometimes presents much more of a problem. Some of them seem meaningless at first, until you tumble to the fact that they are proper names. Take Narutoumi for instance. Naruto is the name of Japan's most famous whirlpool, which is off the coast of Awa, former name of Tokushima Prefecture, in Shikoku. Narutoumi comes, however, not from Awa but from the island of Awaji, between Honshu and Shikoku. He has taken a slight liberty here.

Shinobuyama took his name from Mt. Shinobu, in Fukushima Prefecture, where he first saw the light of day. And Champion Matsunobori's *Matsu* is the first part of the name of his home town, Matsudo, in Chiba Prefecture. Other proper names are contained in Koto-ga-hama (see Plates 3, 18 & 19) and Annenyama. The former comes from Kotohira, in Shikoku; *hama* means "harbor" and the *ga* is merely a connecting link. Annen is the gentleman's surname and all he did was to add *yama*.

The pudgy and popular ex-champion Mitsuneyama, though brought up in Tokyo, originally came from Gumma Prefecture, which boasts the *mitsu* or "three" famed peaks of Myogi, Akagi, and Haruna. And Miyanishiki who, you might think, had some connection with a *miya,* or shrine, was born and raised in the city of Miyako, up north in Iwate Prefecture.

In many cases, however, a wrestler takes his name from the gym to which he belongs. If his name begins with *Toki,* like Tokitsuyama or Tokinishiki, then it may safely be assumed that he's a Tokitsukaze man. Tochinishiki and Tochihikari are obviously disciples of ex-grand champion Tochigiyama, a native of Tochigi Prefecture, whose name since his retirement has been Kasugano. *Tochi* means "horse chestnut," and *hikari,* "light."

Tama-no-umi II belongs to the gym once operated by the late great Grand Champion Tamanishiki. It is of interest to note that the *no* in the middle of his name may be written in *kanji* (Chinese characters) or in the *katakana* syllabary. Originally Tama had it in *kanji,* the same as Tama-no-umi I, presently a TV commentator. But a bad streak brought tears of shame to his eyes, so he changed it to the *katakana* "no." Recently he switched back again. *Tama,* by the way, means "treasure."

Picturesque are the handles adopted by Grand Champion Chiyo-no-yama and ex-grand champion Kagamisato. The former name means "mountain of a thousand eras," and the latter, "village of the Mirror," *kagami* denoting "mirror." Kagamisato's mentor was ex-junior champion Kagamiiwa; it is from him that Kagami took his name. Waka-no-hana means "flower of youth." Waka ("young") is a member of the Hanakago or "basket of flowers" gym. Wakahaguro and Wakamaeda also derive their names from their masters, ex-grand champions Haguroyama and Maedayama respectively.

These are the colorful names the world of Sumo gives its heroes. And what of the fans? What names do they call them? The answer is, they don't. "Ya big bum" has no Japanese equivalent— at least so far as Sumo is concerned.

CHAPTER 14

"Off Duty"

Everything about the Sumo ring is most exotic—the very appearance of the wrestlers, the ceremonial, the posturing, and so on and so forth. One might, then, expect the private lives of the grapplers themselves to be equally exotic, with the great men holding court, surrounded by a bevy of fawning geisha, or having mysterious rendezvous with ladies of gentle birth, and dates with movie stars or glamorous fashion models. Nothing could be farther from the truth.

Your Sumo champion should not be confused with a professional pug in the Western world. The latter frequently becomes the darling of some particular—or should one say not so particular?—social set. He is lionized; he soon embarks on a life of luxury that ill becomes his, in nine cases out of ten, lowly upbringing. The breath of scandal is soon abroad, training is neglected, bouts are lost, and his name quickly forgotten.

Most Sumo men, however, are just plain country fellows when they start out and remain so, as a rule, even when they have reached their destination, the rank of grand champion. To begin with, the young apprentices, novices, scrubs, tyros—call them what you will—have only a very meager amount of pocket money to spend. Their life consists of little other than training, eating, and sleeping, with an occasional visit to a movie theater or a *pachinko* (pinball) parlor. They have neither the time nor the wherewithal to step out of line. As they proceed up the ladder their allowance, or rather salary under the new (1957) system, rises. *Maku-uchi* wrestlers get forty-five thousand yen a month. Not bad, of course, but not enough by any manner of means to play around with.

The majority of wrestlers of *mae-gashira* grade, who are the lower-ranking *maku-uchi,* are still strangers to the bonds of matrimony. Naturally, therefore, they like to step out, and when they do the tab is picked up for the most part by their patrons. Fan clubs are built up around many of the leading wrestlers, and they help to boost a grappler's salary. As in most circles in Japan, it's what one can pick up on the side that really counts. Televiewers must also have noticed elegant geisha scattered here and there in the crowd at a Sumo tournament. These ladies are among the most enthusiastic of all fans, and, quite naturally, the wrestlers reciprocate. Who could be so churlish as to blame them?

Coming to wine—in the broad sense of the term—rumor has it that the demoted, elongated, prognathous ex-champion Ouchiyama is second to none, although ex-grand champion Yoshibayama can give him quite a good run for his money. On the other hand, there are those who have foresworn the demon rum. The handsome Shinobuyama is one, and it's a sure thing his wife is happy. For, in no country more than in Japan do inebriated husbands present such a problem, the more so because usually the wife herself doesn't drink.

Most Sumo men, just as they weigh more and, of course, eat more than you or I, also drink more, on the average. And they always have a perfect alibi, for they can claim, "Oh, we're just drinking to put on weight, highly desirable in a wrestler." As to what they drink, beer's a steady favorite, but a lot of them prefer the local brew, saké, with whisky a very poor third and the others also-rans.

A word or two now as to the big money-earners. Above the *mae-gashira* men are the top-ranking *san-yaku;* among them, *komusubi* and *sekiwake* walk away with a monthly pay check amounting to seventy thousand yen. *Ozeki* can lay claim to a hundred and ten thousand a month, while the men at the top of the tree, the *yokozuna,* bring along a suitcase and cart away a hundred and fifty thousand. With this kind of money they can afford to marry, so it is not surprising that all three of the present grand champions are living in double harness. The champions still enjoying single blessedness are the hirsute Asashio and Koto-ga-hama.

Grand Champion Chiyo-no-yama, who is six feet four inches tall and, with those long arms of his, resembles a giant spider, is married to an Osaka girl, the daughter of a restaurateur. She is as short as he is long. They have, at the moment of writing, one small daughter, and when, after drinking, Papa returns to the nest with the usual present as a peace offering, he invariably wakes up the tot to give it to her. This is considered bad form, but, it is claimed, husband and wife have not had a single quarrel since they were wed.

The Tokyo-born grand champion, Tochinishiki, left the ranks of the bachelors comparatively late. He led his bride, like Chiyo-no-yama's the daughter of a restaurateur, to the altar when he was twenty-nine. They have not, at the moment of writing, been blessed with offspring. Tochinishiki is a great believer in the value of sleep and his wife reports that he even embarrasses her by snoring at the movies. Tochi, however, drinks moderately.

Grand Champion Waka-no-hana, the ever-popular hero of the movie *The Waka-no-hana Story* in which he himself played the leading role, was dealt a cruel blow when his only son, a four-year-old boy, upset a steaming pot of *chanko-nabe,* or wrestler's stew, over himself and was scalded to death. As a consequence, Waka swore off *chanko* for several months, thus weakening himself to such an extent that his form plummeted. The reader may be curious to know what goes into wrestlers' stew. Just about everything, as a matter of fact. Fish, fowl, meat, eggs, vegetables are all tossed in and sugar and soy sauce added. The caloric content must be tremendous.

Champion Matsunobori, he of the bullish mien, was the latest to take to himself a wife, at the advanced age of thirty-two. As with all wrestlers, the affair was arranged through the good offices of a go-between.

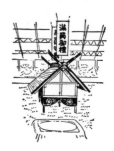

CHAPTER 15

The Charm of Sumo

"Grotesque," one fancies, would be the first epithet to come to a Westerner's mind after his first viewing of Sumo.

And, lacking the patience of the Oriental, he might very well feel inclined to leave it at that, maybe after taking a picture or two for his album. Should he, however, be tempted to give it a second look or a third he would probably change the label. "Bizarre" it might become, or "exotic"; "colorful" perhaps, or even "spectacular."

But first he has a barrier to clear, a stumbling-block that foils a large percentage of non-Orientals, namely the preliminary *shikiri-naoshi* (Plate 2) that precedes the bouts. There are two possible ways of handling this situation. One is to cultivate an interest in the goings-on and try to figure out what it all means; it does mean something, of course, for the men are not going through their routine merely to kill time. The other way is to study the audience.

That fellow in the beret; he's there every day. How can he spare the time? Looks like an artist of some sort. Ah, he's making sketches; must be from some newspaper or other. That girl in *kimono* in the third row, always there, and always alone. What a good-looker! Could be she's a geisha or something; shouldn't be surprised if she was the light of love of one of the wrestlers. Or, televiewers might check their watches and give themselves exactly four minutes. That's how long the wrestlers are allowed for their preliminaries.

Having by this time cleared the hurdle, the Western viewer can sit back comfortably and begin to enjoy the time-honored art. His epithet by now should be "interesting" at least. Or perhaps "quite a show!" And finally, if the thing gets a hold on him, he may find himself muttering "thrilling," "wonderful," even "terrific." If he reaches this exalted stage, he will know wherein the charm of Sumo lies.

In comparing Sumo with allied sports one can see at once why it has, inevitably, a much wider appeal. Take the color, for instance, and the pageantry. There is nothing like it in boxing or in Western-type wrestling. The grunt and groaners, it is true, make a feeble attempt at imitation with the silken gowns they affect as they appear in the ring. But Sumo has the tremendous advantage of a long tradition, which makes all the ceremonial seem not a whit out of place. The ceremonial lends a dignity to the proceedings which is surely one of the principal sources of its charm; without such dignity the label "grotesque" might with justice be applied, as it undoubtedly can to all-in wrestling.

Together with its color and dignity one should note the cleanliness of Sumo, cleanliness in both its literal and figurative senses. Boxing, few would deny, is dirty in both senses of the word, and a boxer, his face smeared with blood and resembling a piece of raw meat, is a most repulsive sight. Blood is seldom drawn in Sumo; if ever it should be, all traces of it are at once removed. As for

fair play, it may be said to be the keynote of Japan's traditional
sport; there is no hitting below the belt. Without a doubt there
are perverted people who are not content unless a certain amount
of dirt is thrown into their sport. Sumo is not for them; they would
be well advised to stick to pro wrestling, where they can have all
the dirt they want.

A Sumo wrestler is a good loser who never betrays dissatisfaction,
whether in word or deed, with the referee's decision. And he is
courteous toward his opponent, however roughly he may be slapped
or flung about. The same applies, with a few rare exceptions, to
rugby football. It should be remembered, however, that most of
the participants in this sport, in Britain at least, come from what
one might term good families. Sumo men, on the other hand, are
in ninety-nine cases out of a hundred the sons of poor farmers or
fishermen, which makes their extreme courtesy and gentleness all
the more remarkable.

In pointed contrast is what goes on at an all-in wrestling bout,
where it is no uncommon thing for the defeated grunt and groaner
to take his beating with such bad grace as to chase the victor outside
the ring and rain blows on him thick and fast, or even pick up a
chair and use it as a weapon. In the case of boxing, the "I wuz
robbed" attitude is too well-known to merit comment. The loser
seldom goes down before a superior opponent; he is beaten by "lousy
refereeing" or "dirty tactics." All this, of course, is considered necessary to whet the appetite of the fans; Sumo can get along very well
without it.

But what, in the opinion of its devotees, constitutes the sport's
greatest charm is the element of drama contained in it. A day's
wrestling at a grand tournament opens with the novices in the early

morning; then, as the afternoon wears on, wrestlers of higher and still higher rank are matched until the show reaches its climax toward evening with the appearance of the grand champions themselves. These, after hours of suspense for the fans, are the final pulsating moments.

And it is not only a single day but the entire fifteen-day tournament that is packed with drama. The interest mounts day by day as candidates for honors drop out one by one until a mere handful are left in contention. As often as not the issue is in doubt until the very last day, which comes to a close with a bout between two grand champions as a fitting finale. The drama ends with the presentation to the victor of the Emperor's Cup and the championship flag and with the playing of the stirring national anthem, the *Kimigayo*.

Index

Other TUT BOOKS available:

Please order from your bookstore or write directly to:

CHARLES E. TUTTLE CO., INC.
Suido 1-chome, 2–6, Bunkyo-ku, Tokyo 112

or:

CHARLES E. TUTTLE CO., INC.
Rutland, Vermont 05701 U.S.A.